FANTASTIC FOUR

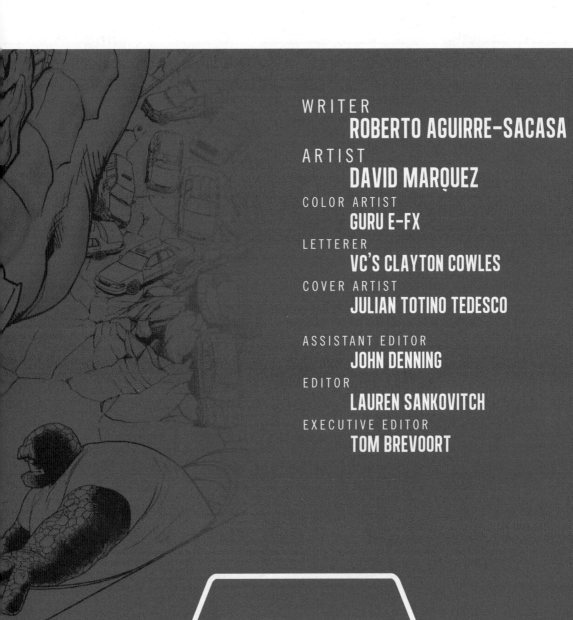

WRITER
ROBERTO AGUIRRE-SACASA
ARTIST
DAVID MARQUEZ
COLOR ARTIST
GURU E-FX
LETTERER
VC'S CLAYTON COWLES
COVER ARTIST
JULIAN TOTINO TEDESCO

ASSISTANT EDITOR
JOHN DENNING
EDITOR
LAUREN SANKOVITCH
EXECUTIVE EDITOR
TOM BREVOORT

SEASON ONE

HERE THEY COME...

SUSAN STORM	JOHNNY STORM	DR. REED RICHARDS	BEN GRIMM
HEART	BODY	MIND	SOUL

SOON, THEY WILL BE...

THE FANTASTIC FOUR

BUT NOT YET.

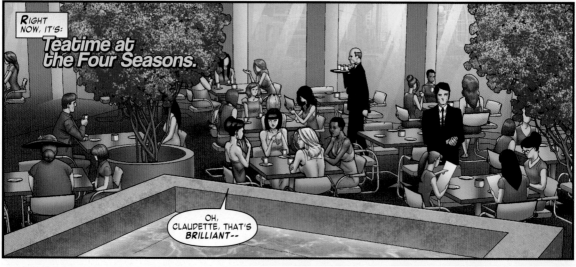

RIGHT NOW, IT'S:

Teatime at the Four Seasons.

OH, CLAUDETTE, THAT'S *BRILLIANT*--

OBVIOUSLY, SPACE TOURISM IS NOT THE GOAL. THE GOAL IS... EVERYTHING ELSE I'M DOING HERE.

SPACE TOURISM IS A *BUSINESS* VENTURE. TO SUBSIDIZE THE REST OF MY WORK.

OUR WORK, REED--MY GOD, YOU'RE INSANE *AND* HUBRISTIC.

IF YOU NEED MONEY, INVENT AN ANTI-AGING SKIN CREAM-- *LITERALLY.*

WHAT ABOUT THE RISKS?

STATISTICALLY, LESS THAN DRIVING A CAR.

ESPECIALLY ON THE VAN WYCK.

JOKE ALL YOU WANT, BUT I'M TRACKING COSMIC STORMS FOR THE NEXT THREE TO EIGHT REVOLUTIONS.

WHY TOMORROW? WHY NOT WAIT?

REED RICHARDS DOESN'T SAY WHAT HE'S THINKING, WHICH IS: BECAUSE I WANT TO BE FIRST.

SO, INSTEAD, HE SAYS NOTHING.

YOU'RE GOING TO BE VILIFIED, YOU KNOW. IF NOT ARRESTED.

YOU DON'T HAVE PERMITS, YOU DON'T HAVE PERMISSION, YOU DON'T HAVE *CLEARANCE--*

WHO'S EVEN *FLYING* WITH YOU?

WHO'S THE MEAT-HEAD?

YOU MESSIN' WITH ME?

DON'TCHA RECOGNIZE DANNY'S BOY?

THAT'S BENJY GRIMM? THE HELL HAPPENED TO HIM?

HUFF--

THUDD

SAME AS HAPPENS TO ALL US PUTZES.

LIFE...

"LIFE HAPPENED TO BEN GRIMM..."

HUFF--

WASN'T HE SOME KINDA FOOTBALL STAR?

LINEBACKER, IN COLLEGE.

AND THEN IN THE ARMY?

AIR FORCE, HIGHLY DECORATED.

OKAY, SO WHAT'S HE TRAINING FOR NOW? A FIGHT?

Ludlow's Garage.

THE CAR IS A BENTLEY. THE MECHANIC IS JOHNNY STORM.

SWEET MARY, I WANT ONE OF THESE.

I'M LOSING YOU, JOHNNY, CAN YOU CHEAT OUT TOWARDS ME MORE?

NOT A PROBLEM. THIS BETTER, ZOE?

MARGINALLY...

LET'S LOSE THE SHIRT.

HAPPY TO, BUT--

--ARE WE *SURE* "SHIRTLESS" IS IN MY CONTRACT?

I HAVE TO SAY, JOHNNY, YOU'RE RIGHT AT HOME IN THIS GARAGE. MOST MODELS, YOU TAKE THEM OUT OF A STUDIO, THEY *FREEZE* UP.

If you've never been, it's hard to explain, but...

Time is...*funny* in space. Different. It expands and contracts like...like *taffy*, almost. While everything else is weightless, it seems to have mass and density...

Space...the universe... the cosmos...containing every possible...*possibility*...

We drift in silence for *moments*; we drift in silence for *days*...

It's amazing to consider: we're four tiny, wonderful, frustrating, marvelous, trivial specimens of human beings on the cusp...

HE MEANS A METRONOME, REED THINKS--

--JUST AS THE *FOUR* FLY INTO ONE OF THE COSMIC STORMS ALYSSA MOY HAD PREDICTED...

We're being *bombarded* by cosmic rays--

BEN, CAN YOU AVERT?

WHAT DO YOU THINK I'M *TRYIN'* TA DO? SUZIE, HANG ON--

TAC-TAC-

THINGS GET...MURKY AT THIS POINT. THEY ALL FOUR REMEMBER THAT *MADDENING* SOUND, ECHOING THROUGH THE SHIP:

-TAC-TAC-TAC-TAC-TAC

THEN...

FOUR:

SO... HOT...

FEELS LIKE I'M BURNING...

ON FIRE...

THREE:

OUR SHIELDING WILL HOLD--

STAY THE COURSE, BEN, AND WE WON'T BREAK--

TWO:

MY EYES...

MY PERIPHERAL VISION...

EVERYTHING'S WHITING OUT...

ONE:

CAN'T... MOVE...

ARMS... TOO... HEAVY...

TRYING... TO GET US... THROUGH...

CONTACT:

ALYSSA, IF YOU CAN HEAR ME, TAKE CONTROL OF THE SHIP--

GET US BACK HOME--

OHMYGOD.

Later.
Ithaca, New York.

LOST CONTACT WITH REED AND THE OTHERS RIGHT BEFORE THE SHIP CRASHED...

SOMEWHERE IN UPSTATE NEW YORK...

SHOULD BE ABLE TO HONE IN ON IT MUCH MORE EASILY--

IT'S A SPACESHIP, FOR GOD'S SAKE...

COSMIC RAYS MUST BE DISTORTING EVERYTHING...

GOD, WHAT IT WOULD MEAN IF THE WORLD LOST A MIND AS EXTRAORDINARY AS REED'S...

Meanwhile.

DON'TBEDEADREED ILOVEYOUREED PLEASEDON'TBEDEAD ORI'LLDIETOO...

LATER, SUSAN STORM WILL REMEMBER THAT HER YOUNGER BROTHER WAS ABOARD THE SHIP, TOO. RIGHT NOW, THOUGH, SHE IS IN DEEP SHOCK, AND HER ONLY THOUGHT IS FOR...

WELL, LET'S THINK ABOUT THAT. ARE YOU IN AGONY? *NO.*

DO YOU SMELL FLESH BURNING? I DON'T *THINK* SO.

IF ANYTHING, YOU SMELL LIKE--

GASOLINE.

MY GOD, JOHNNY, YOU'RE NOT ON FIRE...

...YOU *ARE* FIRE.

WHOA, AND REED'S ALL STRETCHY...

NO KIDDING.

AND, I SUSPECT, LIKE SUE'S INVISIBILITY, YOU CAN SHIFT *BETWEEN* STATES, CONFLAGRATED AND DORMANT--

WAIT, WHAT DO YOU MEAN, *"SUE'S INVISIBILITY?"*

WHAT THE *HELL'S* GOING ON? AND, UHM, WHERE'S BIG, DUMB, AND BEEFY?

...OH. OH, WOW.

WHAT?

WHATEVER YOU DID TA ME, SMART GUY...

BEN--

BEN, *CONTROL YOURSELF*--

WILL DO--

AS SOON AS YER A *PUDDLE*--

IS THAT *REALLY* BEN?

...

WHAT THE HECK DID HE *BECOME*, SUE?

I DON'T KNOW, BUT IT'S *NOT GOOD*, AND HE *BLAMES* REED--

PLEASE--WHATEVER HAPPENED TO YOU--

"*WHATEVER HAPPENED TO ME--*"?!

I TURNED INTA AN *UGLIER* VERSION OF FRANKENSTEIN'S MONSTER--

AND IT'S *YOUR* FLIPPIN' FAULT! MY GUT *TOLD* ME GOING INT'A SPACE WAS A BAD IDEA!

A *SECOND'S HESITATION*, THEN:

WE WERE *ALL* CHANGED, BEN--YOU, ME, JOHNNY, SUE--

BUT SUE CAN PHASE BETWEEN VISIBILITY AND INVISIBILITY--AND JOHNNY CAN CONTROL HIS FLAME (AT LEAST I *THINK* HE CAN)--

HAVE YOU TRIED *WILLING* YOURSELF BACK TO--TO--?

LOOKING *NORMAL?* YEAH, I *TRIED*--

GUESS WHAT, *GENIUS? DIDN'T WORK*--

WHAT ABOUT--?

DEBRIS FROM THE CRASH? I'VE COORDINATED COVERT CLEAN-UP WITH A SECOND TEAM, SO *HURRY UP*--

I'M GETTING IN, BUT THAT *DON'T* MEAN EVERYTHING'S *HUNKY-DORY* NOW--

I'M *STILL*--

EHHH, TAKE IT DOWN A NOTCH, WILL YOU?

REED'LL TURN YOU BACK INTO YOUR *DOUGHY* SELF--

JOHNNY, SHUT UP AND TRADE SEATS WITH ME.

THERE WAS AN EARTHQUAKE IN NEW YORK CITY THIS MORNING, WHICH *MIGHT* KEEP SOME ATTENTION OFF THIS CRASH--

ANOTHER QUAKE? THAT'S... FORTUITOUS.

ALSO, OUR P.R. DEPARTMENT IS FEEDING NEWS OUTLETS CONFLICTING REPORTS ABOUT UFOS, PRIVATE AIRPLANES FLYING OUT OF DESIGNATED AIRSPACE, AND A GOOD-YEAR *BLIMP* GONE ROGUE--

WELL DONE.

I'VE BOUGHT US SOME TIME, THAT'S ALL. THE TRUTH'S GOING TO COME OUT, REED--IT'S JUST A MATTER OF WHEN AND HOW.

BEN--

DON'T CALL ME THAT, SUSIE, I'M *NOT* BEN ANYMORE...

I'M SOME *THING*, BUT I AIN'T BEN GRIMM...

THAT FIRST NIGHT.

LOCKDOWN?!

YOU'VE *GOT* TO BE KIDDING ME! I HAVE A DATE--

SEVERAL DATES, IN FACT--

AND, *UHM,* WHY IS *BEN* EXEMPT? WHY DOES *HE* GET TO GO OUT? HE'S THE ONE WHO LOOKS LIKE MOUNT RUSHMORE! WITH *ACNE!* ON *STEROIDS!*

WE HAVE POWERS WE KNOW *NOTHING* ABOUT, JOHNNY.

UNTIL ALYSSA AND I CAN RUN SOME TESTS, I WANT US ALL TO STAY PUT, OUT OF SIGHT.

BEN, TOO, AS SOON AS HE GETS BACK.

HOW LONG ARE YOU THINKING, REED?

WE-ELL, UNTIL WE CAN ADEQUATELY DETERMINE IF OUR TRANSFORMATIONS ARE PERMANENT OR MUTABLE...

UNTIL WE THOROUGHLY TEST THE LIMITS OF OUR NEW ABILITIES...

UNTIL WE SEE HOW THEY'RE AFFECTING OUR OTHER BIO-SYSTEMS...

THAT SOUNDS LIKE IT'S GONNA TAKE FOR-*FRIGGIN'*-EVER--

A FEW MONTHS, AT LEAST.

EXCUSE ME? DID YOU SAY--?

MONTHS--?!

NO WAY! NO! FLIPPIN'! WAY!!

The Lower East Side.

WHERE DOES BEN GRIMM SPEND HIS FIRST NIGHT AS A MONSTER?

SKULKING IN THE SHADOWS, UP AND DOWN YANCY STREET.

THE OLD NEIGHBORHOOD, WHERE HE GREW UP.

AW, CRIPES...

HAD HIS FIRST KISS HERE...

GOT MUGGED FOR THE FIRST TIME HERE...

HE PLAYED FOOTBALL IN THESE ALLEYS...

MUGGED SOMEONE FOR THE FIRST TIME HERE...

⸮SIGH⸎

GOOD TIMES...

PROBABLY, HE *SHOULD'VE* STAYED IN THE *BAXTER BUILDING* AND LET *REED* RUN HIS TESTS, BUT BEN GRIMM ALREADY KNOWS THE TRUTH, IN HIS *GUT:*

THIS IS HIS LIFE NOW.

REED WILL MAKE PROMISES, OF COURSE. THAT HE WON'T SLEEP UNTIL HE'S FOUND A WAY TO REVERSE THE EFFECTS OF THE COSMIC RAYS, THAT HE'LL DO EVERYTHING IN HIS POWER TO FIX BEN, *BLAH BLAH BLAH...*

PROBABLY, *REED'S* IN KNOTS OVER THIS. *LITERALLY.*

GOOD, BEN GRIMM THINKS. LET 'IM SUFFER. FER ONE NIGHT AT LEAST, LET HIM FEEL CRAPPY.

TOMORROW MORNING, BEN'LL MAKE IT BETTER. HE'LL BE HIS USUAL STAND-UP SELF AND TELL REED *NOT* TO WORRY, THAT HE SHOULD START HIS TESTS. HE'LL TELL SUSIE NOT TO CRY...

HE WON'T TELL HIS OLDEST FRIENDS THE TRUTH. THAT BEN GRIMM IS HOPING HE'S ACTUALLY IN A *COMA,* POST-CRASH, AND THAT THIS IS JUST ONE OF THOSE NIGHTMARES THAT KEEPS GETTING WORSE AND WORSE...

AW, CRUD.

KILL ME NOW...

THE GOOD NEWS IS, YOU'RE NOT *DYING*, I DON'T THINK.

IN FACT, LYS, I'M AFRAID THE *OPPOSITE* IS TRUE. *TO LIVE* IS TO BE IN A CONSTANT STATE OF *DECAY*-- OF BREAKING DOWN. I DON'T BELIEVE I'M *DOING* THAT ANYMORE. WHICH IS... TROUBLESOME.

AGREED.

ON THE OTHER HAND, JOHNNY *MIGHT* BE HYPER-METABOLIZING HIMSELF TOWARDS AN EARLY GRAVE... *OR NOT.*

AND BEN *MIGHT* CONTINUE CALCIFYING INTO A MOTIONLESS, LIFELESS STATUE...*OR NOT.* WHO KNOWS? THEY LEFT BEFORE--

THEY'RE BLOWING OFF STEAM, BUT-- THEY'LL BE BACK.

AS FOR SUSAN...SHE *RESPECTFULLY* DECLINED MY OFFER TO GIVE HER A PHYSICAL.

CAN YOU BLAME HER?

IF YOU'RE IMPLYING SUE'S BEEN *THREATENED* BY ME, OR *JEALOUS* OF ME, SHE *NEEDN'T* BE ANYMORE. YOU'RE BOUND FOR LIFE NOW, THE TWO OF YOU-- THE *FOUR* OF YOU, REALLY.

YOU SURVIVED... I'M NOT EVEN SURE *WHAT*, YET, BUT SOMETHING EXTRAORDINARY.

ME, I'M LIKE THE *FIFTH* BEATLE WHO DIDN'T GET FAMOUS.

SO DO US *BOTH* A FAVOR AND TELL YOUR GIRLFRIEND THAT MY INTERESTS ARE *MERELY* SCIENTIFIC AT THIS POINT.

(ANYWAY, I DON'T WANT TO GO TO BED EVERY NIGHT WITH A MAN WHO *FEELS* LIKE AN INFLATABLE POOL TOY--)

ALYSSA...

...THANK YOU FOR YOUR HELP.

DON'T THANK ME, REED, JUST GIVE ME *ACCESS*.

THERE'S A *BOOK* IN THIS--MAYBE *FOUR* BOOKS--AND I WANT TO...

...WRITE...

WHAT, ALYSSA? WHAT IS IT?

I'M NOT...

FOR A MOMENT, I FELT...

...NEVER MIND. I JUST THOUGHT I HEARD SOMEONE *BREATHING* IN HERE...

SUSAN STORM IS GETTING *BETTER* AT BEING INVISIBLE.

SHE CAN MAINTAIN THE ILLUSION (IF THAT'S WHAT IT IS) FOR *SEVERAL* MINUTES NOW, LIKE-- HOLDING HER BREATH UNDERWATER.

UP NEXT?

FORCE-FIELDS 101...

(ALSO: PUTTING ON SOME CLOTHES.)

The Next Day.

BUSINESS AS USUAL ON THE PUBLIC FLOORS OF THE BAXTER BUILDING.

While Upstairs, in Alyssa Moy's Apartment.

CONSTRUCTION ON THE SECOND AVENUE SUBWAY LINE SUFFERED *FURTHER* SETBACKS LAST NIGHT AFTER YET ANOTHER "SITE-SPECIFIC EARTHQUAKE."

LIVE ON THE SCENE WE HAVE VIVIENNE ROBERTS--

HEL-*LO*, VIVIENNE, *WHAT* IS GOING ON DOWN THERE?

DEPENDS WHO YOU ASK, STEVE. WORKERS IN THE *NEW* SUBWAY'S MAIN TUNNEL ARE DESCRIBING SOMETHING LIKE A MINE COLLAPSE--

NO FATALITIES, BUT *SIX* CITY WORKERS WERE INJURED, WITH TWO EXCAVATORS IN CRITICAL CONDITION AT MERCY GENERAL--

AT LEAST THEY'RE NOT TALKING ABOUT THE CRASH...

GEOLOGISTS FROM EMPIRE STATE UNIVERSITY RECORDED TREMORS STRONG ENOUGH TO HAVE TRIGGERED SUCH A CAVE-IN, BUT AS TO WHAT SPARKED THE TREMORS...WELL, THERE ARE LOTS OF THEORIES, INCLUDING THIS ONE--

LIVING UNDERGROUND, I SEEN A LOTTA THINGS... ALLIGATORS, BLOOD CULTS, CIRCUS FREAKS...BUT NOTHING LIKE WHAT I SEEN TODAY...YOU WANNA KNOW WHAT CAUSED THE EARTHQUAKE?

MONSTERS, LADY, *THAT'S* WHAT--

LIKE GODZILLA, BUT *FREAKIER*...

"THERE YOU HAVE IT, STEVE: MONSTERS IN NEW YORK..."

I MADE YOU SOME COFFEE...

I'M GOOD.

I HEARD YOU COME IN JUST BEFORE DAWN.

DID YOU GET *ANY* SLEEP LAST NIGHT?

WHAT DO YOU THINK?

I THINK... I OWE YOU AN APOLOGY, BEN.

AND A PROMISE. TO DO EVERYTHING I CAN TO MAKE THIS RIGHT.

RIGHT FOR *HIM*, MAYBE, BUT *I'M* GOOD--

IN FACT, I'M *GREAT!*

I SPENT THE NIGHT PRACTICING, AND I GOTTA TELL YOU: THESE NEW POWERS OF MINE WILL *FRY* YOUR MIND--

IS THAT FRESH COFFEE, AWESOME, THANKS--

I SWEAR, JOHNNY...

ALSO, I'VE RECONSIDERED: YOU WANNA DO TESTS, REED? BRING IT. SO LONG AS IT'S *ALYSSA* PROBING ME AND NOT YOU, I'M DOWN WITH WHATEVER.

LITTLE BROTHER, YOU ARE *TRULY* INSUFFERABLE.

FFFZZZTT

MOY HERE, HOLO-CONFERENCING. WE HAVE A GOOD NEWS/ BAD NEWS/GOOD NEWS SITUATION, PEOPLE, SO... PAY ATTENTION.

THE GOOD NEWS IS, NO ONE'S TALKING ABOUT YOU FOUR OR THE CRASH--

THE BAD NEWS IS, THERE'S A MONSTER RAMPAGING IN MIDTOWN--

HOW'S THAT?

DETAILS ARE SKETCHY, BUT APPARENTLY CONSTRUCTION ON THE SECOND AVENUE SUBWAY HAS AWOKEN SOME KIND OF PREHISTORIC MONSTER--

(SOME POOR NEWSCASTER WOMAN WAS JUST EATEN...)

BY ODD COINCIDENCE, IT'S HEADED RIGHT FOR THE BAXTER BUILDING--

THE LAST FEW WEEKS, I HAVE BEEN CHARTING STRANGE SEISMIC ACTIVITY THROUGHOUT THE ISLAND...

AND THIS IS HAPPENING RIGHT NOW?

AS WE STAND HERE WASTING TIME. NEEDLESS TO SAY, THIS PRESENTS A UNIQUE OPPORTUNITY TO GET AHEAD OF THE STORY.

AS WELL AS SAVE LIVES--

HOVERCAR'S FUELED AND IDLING, REED.

THIS IS GOOD, 'CAUSE I WANNA *HIT* SOMETHING-- A *LOT.*

HAVE I MENTIONED I CAN FLY NOW? WELL, I CAN. AND I GOTTA TELL YOU, IT'S *NOTHING* LIKE HOW YOU FLY IN DREAMS--

SUSAN...

...I'M GOING TO NEED YOU TO SIT THIS ONE OUT.

YOUR POWER'S *INVISIBILITY,* NOT *INVULNERABILITY.*

WHAT? ARE YOU *JOKING?*

YOU SAID YOURSELF: WE DON'T KNOW *WHAT* THE FULL EXTENT OF MY POWERS ARE YET.

WHAT BETTER WAY TO TEST THEM THAN OUT IN THE FIELD?

I'M SORRY, BUT UNTIL WE KNOW MORE, I WON'T PUT YOU AT RISK AGAIN--

AND *I'M* SORRY, REED, BUT YOU DON'T GET TO DECIDE THAT--

SUSIE...

...REED'S RIGHT, FER A CHANGE.

LISTEN TO HIM.

STAY HERE, *SAFE,* AND WE'LL BRING YOU BACK A SOUVENIR.

WHAT THE HECK *IS* THAT THING?

OUR TARGET, JOHNNY--

DUH. I *FIGURED*, REED, BUT WHAT *IS* IT?

WHO CARES? LIKE I SAID, I WANNA HIT IT.

GET ME IN CLOSE, STRETCH, AND I'LL *JUMP* ALL OVER ITS--

I THINK, BEN, WE NEED A *SLIGHTLY* MORE EVOLVED PLAN THAN THAT.

OH, YEAH? LIKE WHAT? INVITING IT OVER FOR COOKIES AND *PUNCH?*

NO, LIKE-- JOHNNY, DISTRACT IT. LEAD THE CREATURE AWAY FROM THE CROWDS TOWARDS CENTRAL PARK. WE'LL NEUTRALIZE IT THERE.

GREAT, BUT-- UHM--DISTRACT IT HOW?

FOR PETE'S SAKE, YOU'RE A HUMAN TORCH, JOHNNY, *USE YOUR IMAGINATION*--

RIGHT--

TORCH--

HUMAN--

ME--

GOTCHA--

BEN, I'M TAKING US DOWN. YOU AND I ARE *GROUND SUPPORT.*

CROWD-CONTROL AND BACKUP FOR JOHNNY.

BACKUP FOR JOHNNY? *SHEESH*--

"--HOW THE MIGHTY HAVE FALLEN."

WHAT DO YOU *NEED*, SUSAN? I'M TRYING TO FIND OUT WHAT I CAN ABOUT THIS CREATURE AND FORWARD THE INFORMATION TO REED AND THE OTHERS.

I'VE NEVER THOUGHT OF YOU AS THE STAY-AT-HOME TYPE, ALYSSA.

...

YOU'RE ANGRY BECAUSE, THOUGH REED *CLAIMS* HE'S PROTECTING YOU, IT FEELS LIKE A PUNISHMENT; I UNDERSTAND.

NO DOUBT, TOO, YOU SUSPECT I ADVISED HIM TO SIDELINE YOU; I ASSURE YOU, I *DIDN'T*.

IF THAT'S TRUE, THEN-- *LET'S GET OUT THERE,* ALYSSA!

THIS ISN'T "MAD MEN." WE'RE NOT SECRETARIES; WE'RE NOT WINDOW-DRESSING.

AGREED, BUT A: *I* DON'T WANT TO GET KILLED. AND B: THIS IS WHERE *I* CAN BE MOST HELPFUL.

HOWEVER, IF *YOU* FEEL LEFT OUT...

...LET ME REMIND YOU: THERE'S MORE THAN ONE HOVERCAR IN THE BAXTER BUILDING'S HANGAR.

QUESTION #1: HOW MUCH DOES THE MONSTER WEIGH?

QUESTION #2: HOW STRONG IS BEN GRIMM'S NEW BODY?

AW, MY AUNT PETUNIA...

IDON'T WANNADIE PLEASEDON'TKILLME I'MTOOYOUNG TODIE--

STRONG ENOUGH TO KEEP THIS WOMAN FROM BEING CRUSHED, IT TURNS OUT.

GOTTA TELLYA, LADY: I AIN'T SOME MONSTER BABY--

I MAY NOT LOOK IT, BUT I'M ONE OF THE GOOD GUYS--

PLEASE DON'T EAT ME, MONSTERBABY!

While.

FOLKS, FOLLOW MY ARMS AND THEY'LL LEAD YOU OUT OF THE CREATURE'S PATH--

WHAT THE HELL ARE YOU?

WHAT THE HELL'S HAPPENING?

PLEASE, SIR, TRY NOT TO PANIC--

MY NAME'S DR. REED RICHARDS AND I'M HERE TO HELP.

"HELP"?! "NOT PANIC"?! BUDDY, HAVE YOU SEEN WHAT YOU $%^ING LOOK LIKE?

YOU'RE FREAKIER THAN THE FERRET GUY!

"THE--THE WHO?"

LET THERE BE DARKNESS...

OVERWORLDERS, YOUR CONTINUED ACTS OF TERRORISM AGAINST SUBTERRANEA WILL NO LONGER BE TOLERATED...

ABOVE, THERE IS CHAOS AND CRUELTY AND DISORDER...

UNDER, THERE IS HARMONY, PEACE AND ACCEPTANCE...YOU TRY MY PATIENCE AND FORCE MY HAND...

KORGU IS BUT THE FIRST OF AN ARMY OF MONSTERS BIRTHED IN THE EARTH'S WOMB...ALL UNDER THE MOLE MAN'S CONTROL...

OH, DEAR...

Meanwhile. Above the Mayhem.

THIS IS UN-FRIGGIN'-BELIEVABLE--

KEEP FILMING, JERRY--

PRODUCER CREDIT IF YOU GET ME CLOSE-UPS OF THE MINI-MONSTERS--

"MINI-MONSTERS? I'M COUNTING THREE, JILL--

"THE LAVA GUY--

"THE RUBBER-BAND GUY--

"AND THE BRICK-WALL GUY--"

WHAT ABOUT THE FERRET GUY? ANY SIGN OF HIM?

THE FERRET GUY?

"YEAH, THE STATION'S BEEN GETTING CALLS ABOUT SOME FERRET GUY, TOO--"

RUN, YES... COWER AND SHRIEK, GOOD...

YOU DEVASTATE THE *UNDERWORLD* AS RECKLESSLY AS CHILDREN DIGGING IN A SANDBOX... BUT THERE *WILL BE* A BALANCE...

FOR EVERY *CAVERN*, EVERY SUB-STRATA *CLOISTER* YOU DEFILE, SO SHALL THE MOLE MAN AND HIS CHILDREN TEAR DOWN ONE OF *YOUR* SKYSCRAPERS...

I'VE BEEN MAKING A LIST, DOWN IN THE COLD, DAMP *DARK*...

THE *GREATER* YOUR ARROGANCE AND HUBRIS, THE TALLER AND MORE *AIRBORNE* YOU MAKE YOUR BUILDINGS...

BUT, THEY REST ON FOUNDATIONS OF CLAY...

THE GRAND ACCOUNTING BEGINS *NOW!* WITH *THAT* BRIGHT AND SHINY MONUMENT TO HUMANITY'S FOLLY!

YOU MEAN-- THE BAXTER BUILDING?

MY QUASI-FIANCÉ DESIGNED AND BUILT IT. AND THOUGH I CAN'T DENY HE'S A *SMIDGE* ARROGANT, I'M HOPING *YOU* AND *I* CAN RESOLVE THINGS CIVILLY.

WHAT DO YOU SAY?

YOU... YOU'RE *NOT* RUNNING FROM ME?

DOESN'T LOOK LIKE IT, DOES IT?

MY APPEARANCE... ...IT DOESN'T REVOLT YOU?

HONESTLY? IT *MIGHT* HAVE, TWO DAYS AGO. BUT THAT'S WHEN I WAS *SHALLOW.*

NOW, I'M FINDING IT'S ABSOLUTELY ESSENTIAL TO LOOK *BENEATH* THE SURFACE OF PEOPLE.

I AM ALMOST BLIND, BUT MY OTHER SENSES TELL ME...

YOU'RE A BEAUTIFUL CREATURE.

THANK YOU. MY NAME'S SUSAN STORM.

YOURS ISN'T *REALLY* THE MOLE MAN, IS IT?

N-NO... IT'S... IT'S...

YOU DON'T HAVE TO TELL ME, IF YOU'RE NOT COMFORTABLE.

"I-IT'S HARVEY..."

HERE, GROTTU--

FOLLOW THE FLAMING CARROT--

ALL THE WAY TO CENTRAL PARK, WHICH WE GET TO-- *HOW* AGAIN?

JOHNNY! CAREFUL!

IT'S COOL, REED, I'M TOTALLY--

SZMMMM

≶GASP≶

...DOUSED...

THUNKKK

OH. OH, MY LORD...

SUSAN...

SUZIE-Q...

Y-YES, REED?

YOUR FORCE-FIELDS...

SUSAN, *OPEN YOUR EYES*--

--YOU DID IT, HONEY. YOUR FORCE-FIELDS ARE *MUCH* STRONGER THAN WE ORIGINALLY THOUGHT.

WAS...

...WAS THERE EVER A DOUBT?

UNFORTUNATELY, OUR FRIEND'S *DOWN* BUT NOT *OUT*--

BUT, IF YOU CAN HOLD THE CREATURE IN PLACE, PERHAPS *I* CAN STRETCH MY BODY OVER ITS MOUTH AND NOSTRILS AND DEPRIVE IT OF OXYGEN--

WON'T BE NECESSARY, REED--

OKAY, *THIS* IS EXHAUSTING--

HARVEY? CAN YOU HELP, PLEASE?

CERTAINLY, MISS STORM.

KORGU...

HUHHRR?

...HEEL.

Soon Enough.

THE HECK? "KORGU?!" WHAT KIND OF NAME IS KORGU?

AND, UHM, "HEEL?!"

THAT'S ALL IT TAKES?! SOME WEIRD PENGUIN-GUY SAYING "HEEL?!"

HIS NAME'S HARVEY ELDER, AND HE'S NOT WEIRD, JUST... MISUNDERSTOOD.

YEAH, SO MISUNDERSTOOD HE TRASHED HALF OF NEW YORK...

"HE'S LIVED UNDERGROUND FOR THE LAST SIXTEEN YEARS, JOHNNY. HE'S ANGRY AND HE'S SCARED, BUT HE'S WILLING TO TALK..."

DR. ELDER, I'M REED RICHARDS. WE MET ONCE, BRIEFLY. YOU GAVE A LECTURE AT STATE UNIVERSITY WHEN I WAS A FRESHMAN.

RICHARDS...

I WAS A PRECOCIOUS STUDENT, DOCTOR, AND QUITE SHY.

YES, I VAGUELY REMEMBER A RICHARDS...

SPEAKING HYPOTHETICALLY, DOCTOR. IF I MADE A LAB AVAILABLE TO YOU, WHERE YOU MIGHT SET UP SHOP, SAY, IN THE BASEMENT OF THE BUILDING YOU WERE MOMENTS AWAY FROM KNOCKING DOWN--

--COULD YOU BE PERSUADED TO HELP US BETTER UNDERSTAND YOUR... IDEOLOGY?

I LIVE WHERE THE MOST GLORIOUS MONSTERS DWELL, REED RICHARDS...

WHAT POSSIBLE COMFORT COULD YOU PEOPLE OFFER ME?

HOW 'BOUT...

...MORE MONSTERS, DOC?

HOWDY.

WE'LL BROKER A PEACE BETWEEN OUR WORLDS, HARVEY.

AND MAKE YOU COMFORTABLE, ON *YOUR* TERMS.

THERE WOULD BE CERTAIN REQUIREMENTS...

And So...

...I DON'T KNOW, WE'LL SEE WHAT HAPPENS. FINGERS CROSSED, THOUGH.

IF THE CREATURES *BENEATH* GROUND TRULY DECIDED TO RISE UP AND ATTACK THE CREATURES *ABOVE* GROUND, I DON'T THINK WE'D STAND MUCH OF A CHANCE.

EXCUSE ME--HI--HELLO THERE--

JILLIAN JONES, SPOTLIGHT ON NEW YORK--

THIS IS MY NEWLY PROMOTED *PRODUCER*, JERRY COHEN--

CAN WE STEAL *FIVE* MINUTES OF YOUR TIME?

The Baxter Building, Alyssa Moy.

ROLL WITH IT, REED...PLEASE, GOD...

"...FOR *ONCE* IN YOUR LIFE, JUST *ROLL* WITH IT."

CODE NAMES? THAT IMPLIES--

ROLL WITH IT, HONEY--

WE'RE A *TEAM,* JILLIAN, THE FOUR OF US.

Jillian Jones

Locals Stop Monster

76°
5:05

Latveria, Castle Doom.

MY LIEGE?

FINALLY, RICHARDS *DOES* SOMETHING INTERESTING.

MILDLY.

A TEAM OF, WHAT, SUPER HEROES?

OF ADVENTURERS. EXPLORERS. SCIENTISTS.

AND SUPER HEROES, YEAH--

Jillian Jones

Locals Stop Monster

76°
5:05

WE'RE THE FEARSOME FOUR, PEOPLE!

LEARN TO BURN, SCUM OF THE UNIVERSE!

SUPER-POWERED QUARTET: *Friends or Foes?*

76°
5:05

"FEARSOME FOUR," NOT SURE I LIKE THE SOUND OF THAT...OBVIOUSLY, WE'LL BE CONTINUING TO TRACK THIS STORY AS IT DEVELOPS.

REMINDS YOU OF THE OLD DAYS A BIT--DOESN'T IT, LINDSAY? WORLD WAR II, CAPTAIN AMERICA, THE AGE OF MARVELS...

HAH-HAH-HAH. WOULDN'T KNOW, STEVE. I MEAN, NO OFFENSE, BUT ANYONE CAN SEE I'M FROM A DIFFERENT--SOME MIGHT SAY YOUNGER--GENERATION, SOOO--

CLICKK

Hours Later. The Debate Still Rages.

AAAANND IT'S STILL THE GAFFE HEARD 'ROUND THE WORLD!

PROVIN', YET AGAIN, THAT BEHIND YER PRETTY FACE-- THERE AIN'T NOTHING BUT AIR!

FOR THE MILLIONTH TIME, IT JUST CAME OUT!

AND THERE ARE FOUR OF US...

BUT CRIPES! JOHNNY! THERE ARE SO MANY ADJECTIVES THAT BEGIN WITH F!

THE FORCEFUL FOUR! THE FORTHRIGHT FOUR! THE FORTUITOUS FOUR! HECK, EVEN THE FEARLESS FOUR! TAKE YER PICK!

LAME! LAME! LAME! AND TOTALLY LAME!

AND PEOPLE IN GLASS HOUSES, BENJY! YOU CALLED YOURSELF THE THING! THE THING! IS THAT YOUR CODE NAME? OR YOUR PORN NAME?

--IT DIDN'T MAKE *MUCH* DIFFERENCE.

BETTER?

WELL, AT LEAST NOW YOUR SWELLED HEAD IS ONLY METAPHORIC...

LOOK, REED--

I *SHOULDN'T* HAVE ASKED YOU TO STAY BEHIND, SUE.

THAT WAS... AN ERROR IN JUDGMENT, I *ADMIT* THAT, BUT...I'D LIKE TO MOVE ON NOW, PLEASE.

...

IS THAT AN *APOLOGY?*

SUSAN, BASED ON WHAT I SAW TODAY, YOU *MAY* BE STRONGER THAN THE THREE OF US PUT TOGETHER. *MOREOVER--*

--I DON'T BELIEVE YOU'RE ANYWHERE *NEAR* THE LIMITS OF WHAT YOU'RE CAPABLE OF.

FOR INSTANCE: HAVE YOU TRIED MAKING OBJECTS *OTHER* THAN YOURSELF INVISIBLE?

I... NO, BUT...

WAIT, COULD I *DO* THAT?

POTENTIALLY. WE'LL HAVE TO SEE.

COME CLOSER.

REED... WHAT IS ALL THIS?

SUSAN, PROUST TASTED A BITE OF COOKIE IN A CUP OF TEA AND SAW EVERY ONE OF HIS MEMORIES RISE UP AND THREATEN TO SWAMP HIM...

WE FOUGHT A MONSTER, AND *I* SAW THE FUTURE...

YOU HAD A *PROUSTIAN* MOMENT IN THE MIDDLE OF A J.J. ABRAMS-LIKE *MONSTER* ATTACK?

I SAW WHAT WE *COULD* BECOME...

WHAT WE *NEEDED* TO BECOME...

MY FIRST IMPULSE-- LOCKDOWN--WAS A MISCALCULATION.

OUR DESTINY LIES AHEAD, IN THE FUTURE--FORWARD-FACING, ALWAYS...

"THE DARKNESS...THE *OLD* WAYS...THAT'S FOR *OTHER* MINDS TO CONTEMPLATE..."

WILL THIS SUIT YOU, DR. ELDER?

TOO WARM, MS. MOY...

AND *MUCH TOO* BRIGHT...

OTHERWISE, ASSUMING THE REST OF MY CRITERIA ARE MET, IT *WILL* SUFFICE...

REED... WHAT IS ALL THIS?

SUSAN, PROUST TASTED A BITE OF COOKIE IN A CUP OF TEA AND SAW EVERY ONE OF HIS MEMORIES RISE UP AND THREATEN TO SWAMP HIM...

WE FOUGHT A MONSTER, AND *I* SAW THE FUTURE...

YOU HAD A *PROUSTIAN* MOMENT IN THE MIDDLE OF A J.J. ABRAMS-LIKE *MONSTER* ATTACK?

I SAW WHAT WE *COULD* BECOME...

WHAT WE *NEEDED* TO BECOME...

MY FIRST IMPULSE-- LOCKDOWN--WAS A MISCALCULATION.

OUR DESTINY LIES AHEAD, IN THE FUTURE--FORWARD- FACING, ALWAYS...

"THE DARKNESS...THE *OLD* WAYS...THAT'S FOR *OTHER* MINDS TO CONTEMPLATE..."

WILL THIS SUIT YOU, DR. ELDER?

TOO WARM, MS. MOY...

AND *MUCH* TOO BRIGHT...

OTHERWISE, ASSUMING THE REST OF MY CRITERIA ARE MET, IT *WILL* SUFFICE...

EVERYTHING WE DO FROM NOW ON WILL BE A JOURNEY INTO THE *UNKNOWN*...AN ADVENTURE OF THE *IMAGINATION*...AN EXPLORATION OF THE *INFINITE*...

...WILL YOU JOIN ME, SUSAN?

PLEASE NOTE I'M ASKING *YOU* FIRST.

IT DEPENDS... DO YOU *REALLY* THINK I'M THE MOST POWERFUL?

...

SO LONG AS I CAN STILL BE THE SMARTEST.

DEAL.

THE DESIGN IS SUE'S, THE MATERIAL IS SOMETHING *I* DISCOVERED.

UNSTABLE MOLECULES, WHICH WILL ALLOW *ME* TO STRETCH; SUSAN TO GO INVISIBLE; JOHNNY TO BURN--

--AND ME TA DO A WHOLE LOTTA *NOTHING.*

BEN...

NO OFFENSE TA YER ARTISTIC VISION, SUZIE, BUT FER THE FIRST TIME IN MY LIFE, I GOT ME SOME ROCK-HARD ABS...

...MIND IF I *DISPLAY* 'EM? GIVE THE LADIES A CHEAP THRILL?

WOO-HOO! TAKE IT *OFF,* BENJY!

Two: The Car.

SWEETNESS, REED.

I THINK IT'S SMART WE'RE *BRANDING* EVERYTHING. COPYRIGHT THIS *MERCH.*

GLAD YOU APPROVE OF THE...

..."FANTASTICAR," JOHNNY.

THE-- *WHATWASTHAT UNDERYOUR BREATH?*

ALYSSA'S PUTTING OUT A PRESS RELEASE. *"FEARSOME FOUR"* HAS TOO MANY NEGATIVE CONNOTATIONS--

IS TOO *BAD-ASS,* YOU MEAN.

--SO FROM NOW ON, WE'RE THE *FANTASTIC* FOUR.

WE ARE? JUST LIKE THAT?

SHOULDN'T WE HAVE A MEETING TO DISCUSS IT OR SUMTHIN'?

YES--

--WE *SHOULD.*

CONFERENCE ROOM IN FIVE?

SUE, YOU'RE GOING TO BE THE INVISIBLE WOMAN.

≷SIGH≷ ALREADY AM, ALYSSA.

BEN, PRELIMINARY MARKET RESEARCH ACTUALLY LIKES *"THE THING,"* SO...LET'S GIVE *THAT* A SHOT--

--THOUGH WE CAN ALWAYS RE-EVALUATE LATER.

GOOD THINKIN'.

SWELL.

JOHNNY, CONSIDERING YOUR SIMILARITIES TO THE *ORIGINAL* HUMAN TORCH--

THERE WAS A HUMAN TORCH BEFORE ME?

--WE'RE THINKING THE MOST PRUDENT THING TO DO IS HONOR THAT LEGACY BY CALLING *YOU* THE HUMAN TORCH, AS WELL.

WHAT*EV.*

SO LONG AS I GET AN ACTION FIGURE...

BRILLIANT.

SO WE'LL ANNOUNCE THESE AT THE PRESS CONFERENCE.

WAIT--

HANG ON--

--WHAT'S *YOUR* SUPER HERO NAME, REED?

ELASTIMAN? DR. SILLY PUTTY?

Four: The Debut.

MISTER FANTASTIC--

WASN'T MY IDEA, I SWEAR.

THE INVISIBLE GIRL--

WHAT?! GIRL?!

THE HUMAN TORCH--

PART DEUX.

AND THE THING!

NOW AND FER-EVER.

LADIES AND GENTLEMEN, ON BEHALF OF EVERYONE AT THE NEWLY RENAMED FANTASTIC FOUR, INC., I GIVE YOU THE WORLD'S GREATEST SUPER-TEAM--

"TOGETHER, THEY ARE-- THE FANTASTIC FOUR!"

WOO-HOO! YEAHHH!

THE HUMAN TORCH...

"...MY GREATEST ENEMY..."

...ALIVE?

High Line Park.
Gelato with a Girlfriend.

WE'LL FIGHT CRIME, NANCE, IF WE SEE IT, BUT WE DON'T GO OUT ON NIGHTLY PATROLS OR ANYTHING--

RIGHT, BECAUSE *THAT* WOULD BE WEIRD.

WELL, MAYBE JOHNNY DOES, BUT ALL HE READS ARE *COMIC BOOKS*--

INCOMING, BY THE WAY.

...WE'RE NOT SUPER HEROES *PER SE*, SINCE WE DON'T HAVE SECRET IDENTITIES.

NOT THAT YOU *NEED* A SECRET IDENTITY TO BE A SUPER HERO, BUT THE TWO *DO* SEEM LINKED.

UH-*HUH*. AND YOU HAVE *TIGHTS*.

INVISIBLE WOMANCANIHAVE YOURAUTOGRAPH? TOMELVIN PLEASE?

OHMYLORDIE ICAN'TBELIEVEIT'S REALLYYOU!

ABSOLUTELY. HAPPY TO. I JUST HAVE TO ASK--

--THERE ISN'T *DISAPPEARING* INK IN THIS PEN, IS THERE?

SHTICK. YOU HAVE A *SHTICK* NOW...

UN-REAL.

OHMYGODILOVEYOU THANKYOUIWILL NOTSELLTHISON EBAYISWEAR.

WE DID LETTERMAN AND *THE DAILY SHOW*, BUT I DOUBT THAT'S GOING TO BE A REGULAR THING--

THOUGH JOHNNY *IS* THE MOST TWITTERED-ABOUT PERSON ON THE PLANET RIGHT NOW--

UGH, ALL THESE PEOPLE STARING AT US, HOW DO YOU HANDLE IT?

EASY.

...RIIIIGHT. INVISIBILITY.

JUST 'TIL WE FIND AN OUT-OF-THE-WAY CORNER.

...

WELL, AND WHAT ABOUT REED? HOW'S *THAT* BEEN?

"SERIOUSLY, NANCE? I LOVE YOU, BUT YOU'RE CRAZY..."

Clinton Castle, Battery Park.

TO THE PEOPLE AROUND HIM, HE LOOKS LIKE ANY OTHER MEMBER OF NEW YORK'S DISENFRANCHISED CLASS.

ONE OF THE NAMELESS AND VOICELESS WHO HAUNT THE CITY'S ALLEYWAYS AND HOMELESS SHELTERS, DERELICT DOORWAYS AND ABANDONED BUILDINGS.

STAND DOWN, NAMOR!

KNEEL, TORCH! BOW BEFORE ME!

ONE OF THE THOUSANDS WHO DIDN'T MAKE IT, WHO SLIPPED THROUGH THE CRACKS, WHO SAW THEIR DREAMS CRUSHED.

THOUGH THIS PARTICULAR GENTLEMAN DOESN'T DREAM THE USUAL DREAMS. OF STARDOM, FINANCIAL SUCCESS, INSTANT CELEBRITY. HE DREAMS, INSTEAD, OF...

WATER! TRUMPS! FLAME!

...CORAL CITIES...

...AND TENTACLED PETS...

...AND STOLEN KISSES ENJOYED UNDER STARLIKE SCHOOLS OF LUMINESCENT FISH...

HE DREAMS OF A PLACE THAT ONLY EXISTS IN LORE AND FABLE. (NO! REAL! IT WAS REAL!) A KINGDOM CALLED ATLANTIS...

I WAS A PRINCE ONCE...

I FOUGHT A MAN MADE OF FIRE, WHO LIVES AGAIN...

HEEEY, MACIN? YOU OKAY THERE, BUDDY?

YOU'RE NOT GONNA JUMP, ARE YA?

HIS FRIENDS--IF THAT'S WHAT YOU WOULD CALL THE MEN HE'S SPENT YEARS (DECADES?!) HUDDLING WITH AGAINST THE WINTER'S CHILL (THOUGH HE, HIMSELF, NEVER FELT THE COLD)-- CALL HIM "MACIN," BUT...

THAT IS NOT MY NAME, MONKEY.

HOW-- HOW'S THAT?

MY NAME--

--IS NAMOR!

RRENNNNCCHHH

HE HAS THE **SHAPE** OF A MAN.

THE **GAIT** OF A MAN.

FETCH! DUSTY, **FETCH!**

THE **SPEECH** OF A MAN.

WHEN HE CLOSES HIS EYES AND SLEEPS...

...BEN GRIMM IS **STILL** A MAN.

THE **CARRIAGE** OF A MAN.

OH, HEY, SORRY ABOUT THAT--

⸘HEH⸘ GUESS I DON'T KNOW MY OWN **STRENGTH.** AND DUSTY--WELL, HE CAN BE...A LITTLE **OVEREAGER**, SOMETIMES.

THE **DREAMS** OF A MAN...

IT'S ALL RIGHT. OBVIOUSLY IT WASN'T INTENTIONAL, AND IT'S NOT LIKE ANYONE DIED, SOOOOO... ...WELL, **HERE.** SINCE I CAN'T GIVE YOU YOUR LIFE BACK, I'LL AT LEAST GIVE YOU YOUR STICK.

UHHMM...

BEN! YO, FUGLY, WAKE UP!

THE HECK?! SUZIE--?

UHHH, GUESS AGAIN, ROCK-FER-BRAINS.

CRIMINIES, JOHNNY, FER A SECOND I THOUGHT--

UGHHH, NEVERMIND...

OH, MY GOD, WERE YOU DREAMING ABOUT MY SISTER?

IF SO, YOU ARE A PERV. IF NOT, YOU STILL ARE.

AND YOUR EXCLAMATIONS OF SURPRISE? NEED UPDATING. "CRIMINIES"? WHO SAYS "CRIMINIES" ANYMORE?

SHUT IT, JOHNNY, OR I'LL SHUT IT FOR YOU.

I WAS DREAMING ABOUT...

CONEY ISLAND, WHERE I SPENT MY SUMMERS, LIFEGUARDING AND HITTING ON GIRLS--

DUSTY, THE DOG I HAD GROWING UP ON YANCY STREET, WHO DIED WHEN A CAR HIT 'IM, WHEN I WAS FRIGGIN' TWELVE--

...EHHHHH, SKIP IT. WHATTYA WANT?

AND YEAH, JUNIOR, YOUR SISTER SUE. THE ONE GAL I DIDN'T MESS WITH IN COLLEGE, 'CAUSE MY BEST FRIEND LOVED HER--

"I THINK YER NUTTIER THAN A *FRUITCAKE*..."

Meanwhile...

IT DOES NOT TAKE THE SUB-MARINER LONG TO GET HOME.

HE IS, AFTER ALL, THE PLANET'S FASTEST SWIMMER. AND HE RIDES THE OCEAN'S THERMAL CURRENTS AS EASILY AS--

N-NO. IT *CANNOT* BE...

SIXTEEN HUNDRED FATHOMS BELOW, NAMOR *BARELY* FEELS THE OCEAN'S DEVASTATING PRESSURE--

--YET HIS HEART IS *CRUSHED* BY WHAT HE FINDS WHERE THE SPIRES AND DOMES OF ATLANTIS ONCE LOOMED.

A CITY-- A CONTINENT-- IN RUINS...

SUCH DEVASTATION, HE THINKS. LIKE POMPEII...

BUT THE VOLCANO *VESUVIUS* DESTROYED THAT CITY, AND *THIS*--

--THIS RUINATION, NAMOR KNOWS, COULD ONLY HAVE BEEN WROUGHT BY *ONE* SPECIES...

HAROLD ALDER THOUGHT HE WOULD TAKE A STROLL BY THE WATER DURING HIS LUNCH BREAK. (A FATEFUL DECISION THAT MIGHT COST HIM HIS LIFE.)

WHA--WHA--WHA--WHA--WHAT?!

ATLANTIS, MONKEY! WHAT DID YOUR PEOPLE DO TO IT?!

I-- I--I-- I HAVE NO IDEA WHAT YOU'RE TALKING ABOUT--

MY KINGDOM, MONKEY! WHAT-- HAPPENED-- TO--

"ATLANTIS" DIDJA SAY?

WE WERE JUST THERE...

WHAT?

AFTER WE CRASHED IN ITHACA, ALYSSA RECOVERED THE REMAINS OF OUR SHIP. EVEN MORE THAN US, *ITS* HULL ABSORBED THE WORST OF THE STORM'S RAYS.

EXHIBIT-A, BEN. WE HYPER-COMPRESSED THE DEBRIS INTO A CUBE OF METAL *TEEMING* WITH COSMIC ENERGY. LIKE A... SYNTHETIC METEOR, ALMOST.

IN THIS FORM, WE CAN HARNESS AND MANIPULATE THE METAL'S RADIATION. SLIDE IT ALONG A SCALE, IF YOU WILL--

IMAGINE TUNING A RADIO...

--AND *RE*-IRRADIATE YOU, BEN--

AND...I'LL GO BACK TO MY CUTE, LOVABLE, CUDDLY SELF?

HARD TO PREDICT, BUT THERE'S A CHANCE OF THAT, YES.

THAT *IS* THE HOPE.

CONVERSELY--

...MAYBE MAKE ME WORSE.

CONVERSELY, COSMIC ENERGY IS... *DIFFICULT* TO PREDICT. (UNDERSTATEMENT OF THE MILLENNIUM.) RE-EXPOSURE MAY *"CURE"* YOU, BEN, OR HAVE *ZERO* EFFECT, OR...

THE ETERNAL CONUNDRUM, MR. GRIMM. THE LADY OR THE TIGER, WHICH SHALL IT BE?

THE CHOICE IS YOURS, BEN.

OF COURSE WE'LL DO WHATEVER YOU WANT.

WHAT C'N I SAY? MRS. GRIMM'S BOY'S FEELING *LUCKY.* CRANK THIS TUB *UP--*

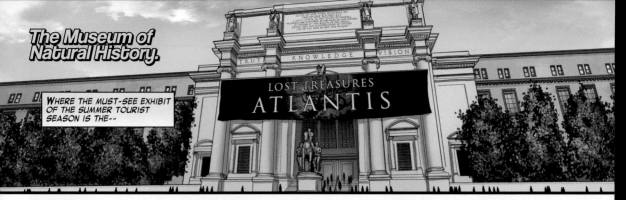

The Museum of Natural History.

LOST TREASURES
ATLANTIS

WHERE THE MUST-SEE EXHIBIT OF THE SUMMER TOURIST SEASON IS THE--

OHMYGRACIOUS! THAT MAN IS PRACTICALLY IN THE NUDE!

I AM SO MOVING TO NEW YORK THE SECOND I GRADUATE.

FILTHY MONKEYS...

UNSPEAKABLE, HE THINKS.

ATLANTIS SACKED AND HER TREASURES ON DISPLAY LIKE A HARLOT'S GLASS JEWELS.

INCLUDING:

THE HORN OF PROTEUS...

THE TRUMPET OF GLAUCUS...

AND THE MONKEYS DO NOT EVEN RECOGNIZE IT FOR WHAT IT IS...

GOOD ASSUMPTION, ZOE.

THAT'S AGENDA ITEM NUMBER--

--BRRRRZZHHHOHNNY? DIDN'T YOU GET THE ALERT?

UH, LITTLE BUSY RIGHT NOW, SIS--

SO I'M GATHERING--

SORRY TO INTERRUPT--

ZOE, WAS IT? I CAN NEVER KEEP TRACK--

BUT SOME LUNATIC IN A SPEEDO JUST ROBBED THE NATURAL HISTORY MUSEUM AND MY BROTHER AND HIS TESTOSTERONE ARE NEEDED--

HOW IS THIS AN FF PROBLEM? SOUNDS LIKE A FRATERNITY PRANK TO ME. AND I, OF ALL PEOPLE, WOULD KNOW--

"WE-ELL, JOHNNY. AFTER THE LUNATIC IN A SPEEDO STOLE SOME KIND OF...ATLANTEAN MUSICAL INSTRUMENT, HE BUSTED THROUGH THE MUSEUM'S ROOF AND APPARENTLY FLEW TOWARDS THE ATLANTIC OCEAN..."

LEVIATHAN, HEAR THE TRUMPET...

...AND RISE!

"SO HE'S SOME KIND OF SUPERHUMAN, GOT IT, OKAY."

FA-WHOOOOOOOOOO~

SO YOU WANT ME TO-- OHMYGOSH, *JUST* REALIZED--

HOW'S THE *WHALE*, SUE?

THE *WHAT* NOW? THE *WHAT* NOW?

THE LIFE-SIZE WHALE IN THE MUSEUM'S MAIN HALL--

THE ONE I WAS *OBSESSED* WITH AS A KID--'MEMBER I USED TO MAKE MOM AND DAD TAKE US, LIKE, *EVERY DAY?*

VAGUELY--

LISTEN, JOHNNY, I'M IN THE FANTASTICAR, HEADING TOWARDS YOU. I CAN *TRY* AND GET A SIT-REP ON THE WHALE, BUT--

DON'T BOTHER, THIS IS *PERSONAL* NOW--

SORRY, ZOE, *TORCH-TIME.*

HOW *DARE* YOU? AND HOW AM I SUPPOSED TO GET *DOWN?*

PLEASE, SOME FLYING DUDE IN UNDERWEAR? TEN MINUTES, TOPS.

"WHAT ABOUT STRETCH ARMSTRONG AND THE GREAT WALL OF CHINA, SUE?"

"I TRIED THEM, BUT THEY'RE HOLED-UP IN REED'S LAB. AGAIN. WORKING ON SOMETHING QUOTE/UNQUOTE 'EXTREMELY IMPORTANT.' AGAIN. PROBABLY A NEW VERSION OF ROCKY ROAD ICE CREAM..."

THIS IS AGONY, ALYSSA.

THIS IS SCIENCE, REED.

IRRADIATION ALMOST COMPLETE, BY THE WAY.

TAC-TAC-TAC-TAC-TAC-TAC-TAC-TAC-TAC

INSIDE THE "STORM CHAMBER," BEN GRIMM KEEPS HIS EYES CLOSED, AS INSTRUCTED.

HE FEELS SOMETHING LIKE... WARM SAND SPILLING ALL OVER HIS BODY, LIKE WHEN HE USED TO BURY HIMSELF AT THE BEACH, AS A BOY.

HE FEELS HEAVIER, THEN LIGHTER...

TIME SEEMS TO SLOW... STOP...REASSERT ITSELF...

TAC-TAC-TAC-TAC-TAC-TAC-TAC-TAC-TAC

IT GETS DARK BEHIND HIS EYELIDS, THEN...LESS DARK...

THAT SOUND--THAT DAMN, MISERABLE SOUND-- DWINDLES TO A TRICKLE...

TESTS. WE-- WE NEED TO RUN *TESTS*, REED. BEFORE WE DO *ANYTHING* ELSE.

AGREED. AND WE WILL, ALYSSA, BUT FIRST--

--HOW DO YOU *FEEL*, BEN?

HOW DO I *FEEL*? BUDDY, YOU GAVE ME MY *LIFE* BACK! I FEEL LIKE-- *LIKE*--

BRZZZZZRT--

--LIKE *FRIGGIN'* KISSING YOU!

BEN--

YOU'RE SHIRTLESS AND THIS IS MAKING ME *EXTREMELY* UNCOMFORTABLE--

HANG ON, SOMETHING--

SOMETHING'S HAPPENING...

I WANNA EAT SUMTHIN'-- *ANYTHING!* I WANNA GET A--A *MASSAGE!* I WANNA--

--I WANNA GO TO THE BEACH AND GET *SUNBURNED!* I WANNA--

ALYSSA?

"I'M RECEIVING BITS AND PIECES FROM THE C.P.U. OF SUE'S *FANTASTICAR*. SOMETHING TO DO WITH THE *SUPERHUMAN* SHE WAS CALLING ABOUT EARLIER..."

FASCINATING CREATURE, YOUR BEAUTY *AROUSES* ME--

ARE YOU THE TORCH'S *MATE?*

WHOEVER HE IS, HIS BODY'S STRAIGHT OUT OF A ZACH SNYDER MOVIE--

H-HIS *SISTER*, ACTUALLY...

NAMOR, RIGHT?

A.K.A. THE SUB-MARINER? A.K.A. IMPERIUS REX? A.K.A. PRINCE OF ATLANTIS? JOHNNY STORM, BIG, *BIG* FAN!

I USED TO READ COMIC BOOKS ABOUT YOU WHEN I WAS KID--

OKAY, EVEN AS RECENTLY AS LAST WEEK--

DIDN'T YOU *DISAPPEAR* OR SOMETHING?

YOU SEEM MORE *EVOLVED* THAN THE REST OF YOUR PITIABLE RACE, BEAUTY. *PERHAPS* I'LL LET YOU LIVE--

TAKE YOU AS A WIFE--

"HIS EYES," SHE THINKS, "HYPNOTIC, ALMOST...

"NOT TO MENTION HIS ABS...

"THOUGH I'M *NOT* LOVING HIS TONE, AND HE SEEMS ACTUALLY, *POSSIBLY*, MORE CHAUVINISTIC THAN REED, EVEN--"

"LET... ME...LIVE?"

HA-HA, OH-KAY, YOU'RE *SAYING* THINGS--

AND I'M *HEARING* THEM--

BUT I HAVE *NO CLUE* WHAT YOU'RE TALKING ABOUT--

THEN I WILL *EXPLAIN* IT TO YOU, TORCH--

JOHNNY--

YOUR PEOPLE *DECIMATED* ATLANTIS--

THEN PLUNDERED AND DISPLAYED HER TREASURES FOR *SPORT*--

"SO FAST," SHE THINKS, "HOW CAN HE MOVE SO--?"

YOU'LL *DROWN,* TORCH, *ALL* OF YOU--

--BUT *YOU* FIRST.

DUDE, YOU ARE *SO* MUCH LESS COOL THAN YOUR COMIC BOOK COUNTERPART--

AND WHAT'S WITH THAT *RIDONKULOUS* BEARD?

DIE, TORCH!

DROWN IN MY *VENGEANCE!*

HE WILL, UNLESS--

BUBBLE.

WHAT--
--WHAT *DEVILRY* IS THIS?

INVISIBLE AIR BUBBLE. *WELL* DONE, SIS...

I'D ASK YOU WHAT *ROCK* YOU'VE BEEN LIVING UNDER, BUT IT OCCURS TO ME THAT'S PROB'LY *EXACTLY* WHERE YOU'VE BEEN, HUH?

SO LET'S *BURN* SOME OF YOUR CONFUSION AWAY, WHATTYA SAY?

AND MAYBE SOME OF THAT EXCESS HAIR.

MONKEY, YOU ARE *OUT* OF YOUR ELEMENT--

WHAT CAN A MAN OF FIRE *POSSIBLY* DO AGAINST THE PRINCE OF ATLANTIS WHILE SURROUNDED BY *WATER?*

"SO LONG AS SUE KEEPS CONCENTRATING--

GO SUPER-NOVA, JOHNNY--

"--YEAH, EXACTLY, I CAN GO SUPER HERO-NOVA ON YOUR FISH BUTT, NAY-NAY."

FWOOHMMM

THE TORCH'S FIRE FLARES HOT AS A VOLCANO'S CORE--

"IF NAMOR GETS THEM UNDERWATER, JOHNNY AND SUE ARE *DOOMED*--"

ALSO STREAMING YOUR WAY: *EVERYTHING* WE HAVE ON NAMOR--BOOKS, PROFILES, EYEWITNESS ACCOUNTS, *MILITARY FILES*--

HIS POWER LEVELS ARE OFF THE CHARTS AND HE HAS A *GRUDGE* AGAINST SURFACE DWELLERS AS *DEEP* AS THE *ATLANTIC*--

REED-- BUDDY--*WHAT* CAN I DO?

IN YOUR CURRENT HUMAN STATE? UNFORTUNATELY *NOTHING*, BEN--

PRAY--

"*PRAY* THAT JOHNNY AND SUE ARE STILL ALIVE SOMEHOW--"

OH, LORD...

WHAT IS IT, ALYSSA-- NAMOR?

NO, REED, SOMETHING-- *BIGGER*...

BUT, I'M SURE, NAMOR- RELATED...

AW, CRUD...

YOU'RE NOT "SITTING THE FIGHT OUT," BEN, IT'S JUST NOT YOUR FIGHT ANYMORE--

DUE RESPECT, DR. MOY, THAT'S *CRAPOLA*--

IF SUSIE, MATCHSTICK, AND STRINGBEAN ARE IN TROUBLE--

THEY'LL HAVE TO TAKE CARE OF THEMSELVES--

YOU HEARD REED. IN YOUR HUMAN FORM, YOU'D BE A LIABILITY--

YEAH, I *HEARD*--

MESSAGE RECEIVED, *LOUD AND CLEAR*--

HOW LONG DOES IT TAKE TO BUILD A LIFE...? YEARS? DECADES?

TRY MINUTES, SECONDS. TO IMAGINE...

YOURSELF GETTING MARRIED TO A NICE GIRL FROM QUEENS, MEBBE...

BUYING A HOUSE, IN RIVERDALE OR LONG ISLAND CITY...

GROWING OLD TOGETHER, ENJOYING EACH OTHER'S COMPANY, RAISING A FAMILY...

IN THE SHORT TIME HE'S BEEN HUMAN AGAIN, BEN GRIMM HAS IMAGINED-- *BUILT*--LIFE AFTER LIFE, DOZENS OF POSSIBILITIES... ALL OF THEM *GOOD*, ALL OF THEM *WORTHY*...

THE THING IS...

THE *LITERAL* AND *METAPHORIC* THING IS...

THOSE AIN'T MY LIFE.

BEN...?

AND I DON' NEED TA *MAKE UP* A FAMILY, I ALREADY *GOT* ONE, AND THEY NEED ME...

JOHNNY AND SUSIE, THEY COULD BE HURT OR-- OR WORSE...

BEN, WHATEVER YOU'RE THINKING, YOU NEED TO *STOP* THINKING IT RIGHT NOW--

WE CHANGED YOU BACK ON THE *LONGEST* OF LONG-SHOTS, A *HAIL MARY PASS*--

IF WE TRIED TO CHANGE YOU AGAIN, IT COULD A: KILL YOU; OR B: TURN YOU INTO SOMETHING *WORSE*--

OR C: *NOTHING* MIGHT HAPPEN, RIGHT?

DON'T MATTER, DOC, WE GOTTA TRY...

I-- I *WON'T* DO IT--

YOU CAN'T OPERATE THE STORM CHAMBER, AND I--I *REFUSE* TO--

REED WOULD KILL ME, AND I WOULDN'T BE ABLE TO *LIVE* WITH MYSELF--

AIN'T YOUR CHOICE, DOC, BUT IF YOU WON'T--

--WILL *YOU*, MOLE-Y?

...

SCIENCE *IS* RISK, MS. MOY, AND EVERY SECOND THAT PASSES, MY PHOBIA OF A PLANET ON WHICH WATER RULES EARTH *DEEPENS*...

MOREOVER, HOW COULD I, THE MOLE MAN, DENY A MONSTER HIS TRUEST WISH?

YES, MR. GRIMM, I'LL HELP YOU.

...

TRY NOT TA WORRY, DOC. MORE'N ANYTHING, BEN GRIMM LISTENS TO HIS *GUT*. AND RIGHT NOW, HIS GUT IS YELLING *REAL LOUD*--

"THE FANTASTIC FOUR DON'T WORK IF IT AIN'T *FOUR*, MEATHEAD!"

Meanwhile. Finally.

VISUAL CONTACT, ALYSSA--

NAMOR!

?

MY NAME IS REED RICHARDS OF THE FANTASTIC FOUR. WHATEVER GRIEVANCES YOU HAVE, I *SWEAR* I'LL HELP YOU RESOLVE THEM, BUT FIRST YOU NEED TO TELL ME-- *WHERE ARE SUSAN AND JOHNNY STORM?*

THE TORCH AND HIS SISTER?

THEY DEFIED ME, SO I KILLED THEM.

WHAT?

I SEARCHED THE OCEAN FOR THEIR CORPSES--TO SEND TO YOUR RACE AS A *WARNING*-- BUT ALREADY THEY'VE BEEN SUCKED AWAY BY THE TIDES...

WHY, WERE THEY IMPORTANT TO YOU?

YES, BUT THAT'S PRESSURE FROM THE *OUTSIDE*, RIGHT?

WHAT WOULD HAPPEN IF I IMAGINED AN INVISIBLE BUBBLE *INSIDE* YOUR THROAT...

...THEN STARTED TO *EXPAND* IT?

SUSAN--

MUCH AS I *WANT* TO BE SUPPORTIVE--

ESPECIALLY RIGHT AT THIS MOMENT--

WE NEED NAMOR ALIVE TO CALL OFF HIS "LEVIATHAN"--

HISWHATNOW?

ALMOST DRY, BY THE WAY--

NOT AND, IN FACT, *CANNOT*.

I *WOULD*

THE TRUMPET OF GLAUCUS HAS BEEN SOUNDED. LEVIATHAN HAS BEEN AWOKEN. AS SURE AS DAY FOLLOWS NIGHT--

--YOUR NEW YORK *WILL* BE DESTROYED.

IS *ALREADY* BEING, I IMAGINE.

REED, WHEN I WAS UNDERWATER, LOOKING FOR JOHNNY...

...I SAW *THIS*, TOO.

SEEMED LIKE IT MIGHT BE USEFUL...

... WE'LL TAKE IT AND NAMOR WITH US--

"--AND HOPE, BY SOME MIRACLE, THERE'S *STILL* A NEW YORK TO SAVE WHEN WE GET THERE."

Battery Park.

LEVIATHAN HAS RISEN.

AND IT KNOWS ONLY ONE IMPULSE: TO DESTROY, ON LAND AS IN THE SEA...

IT DOES NOT THINK, BUT IF IT DID, IT WOULD BE THINKING: THIS FORT FIRST.

HEY, UGLY-- HANDS OFF AND GUESS WHAT?

HHHURGGH?

IT'S CLOBBERIN' TIME, PRECIOUS.

RRRUUHHHHRRRRR...

RRHHHAARRRRHHH!

YEAH, YEAH, YEAH, THE LINE HOLDS HERE--

AS LONG AS I'M BREATHING, YOU AIN'T HURTING ANYONE--

--AREN'T SURE HOW LONG THE BATTLE'S BEEN RAGING, BUT THE FANTASTIC FOUR'S THING HAS SO FAR MANAGED TO MATCH THE SEA CREATURE BLOW FOR BLOW, FIGHTING IT TO A SEEMING STANDSTILL--

Jillian Jones   MONSTER MAYHEM CONTINUES!   74° 2:11

DOWN, DAMMIT--

GO-- DOWN--

--MAYOR HAS DECLARED A STATE OF EMERGENCY AND BEGUN TO EVACUATE THE CITY, BUT HOW MUCH TIME WILL THE THING BE ABLE TO BUY NEW YORK'S CITIZENS?

BATTERY PARK BATTLE RAGES; NYC WAR ZONE!   74° 2:11

GOTTA--

STAY TOUGH--

CAN'T--

GIVE UP--

--AND, OF COURSE, THE BIG QUESTION IS: "WHERE'S THE REST OF THE FANTASTIC FOUR?"

HOW MUCH LONGER TILL THE CAVALRY ARRIVES?

BEN! REEDSAIDYOU WEREHUMANAGAIN BUTTHENALYSSAJUST CALLEDANDSAIDYOUWEREN'T SOI'MALLCONFUSED, BUTDOMEAFAVORAND BACKOFF'CAUSEREED SENTMEAHEADTOTRY SOMETHING--

FANTASTIC THREE MISSING IN ACTION?

THE HUMAN TORCH BLOWS THE TRUMPET OF GLAUCUS, THEN--

--AS BEFORE...AS ALWAYS...LEVIATHAN IS COMPELLED TO ANSWER. AND FOLLOW.

⸮HEH⸮

I...SOFTEN'D HIM...UP...FER YOU...

"IF LEVIATHAN RESPONDS, KEEP BLOWING AND KEEP FLYING," REED SAID. "BE THE PIED PIPER, JOHNNY--

"LEAD HIM AWAY FROM MANHATTAN AND OUT TO SEA--

"--UNTIL HE DISAPPEARS UNDER THE WAVES AND IS BACK WHERE HE BELONGS, HIBERNATING AT THE OCEAN'S BOTTOM..."

Back on Land.
The First of Many Questions:

BEN, *WHAT* IN GOD'S NAME HAPPENED?

MOLE MAN LENT ME HIS MONSTER...

EVERYTHING ELSE, I C'N EXPLAIN...

I'LL BREAK OUT OF THIS PRISON, BEAUTY.

IT'S *SUSAN*, AND--I DON'T THINK SO.

TRY HITTING THAT GLASS REED INVENTED--*ESPECIALLY FOR YOU*--AND *SEE* WHAT HAPPENS. YOUR BLOWS WILL AMPLIFY AND ECHO BACK AT YOU, TURNING YOUR BRAIN INTO SO MUCH MUSH.

WHICH, IN YOUR CASE, WOULDN'T MAKE MUCH DIFFERENCE.

GET *COMFORTABLE*, PRINCE. YOU'RE THERE UNTIL WE FIND THE MISSING ATLANTEANS AND THEN FIGURE OUT, TOGETHER, HOW TO PUNISH YOU FOR YOUR CRIMES--*LONG-TERM*.

YOU WANTED ME. I SAW IT IN YOUR EYES.

WHOA.

PLEASE. YOU'RE HANDSOME, NAMOR, BUT A PIG.

AND I'LL TELL YOU THE SAME THING I TELL MY GIRLFRIENDS: *YES*, REED AND I *ARE* DIFFERENT, AND YES, HE'S OVER-PROTECTIVE OF ME, AND *YES*, HE CAN BE REMOTE, ALOOF, *WHATEVER* YOU WANT TO CALL IT; AND *YES*, WE'LL PROBABLY *NEVER* GET MARRIED--BUT THE HEART WANTS WHAT THE HEART WANTS...

"...AND *MY* HEART WANTS REED RICHARDS. ALWAYS HAS, ALWAYS WILL."

...HARVEY'S *THRILLED* TO HAVE HELPED SECURE EARTH'S, UH, "SUPREMACY OVER WATER." AND ALYSSA'S STILL DISTRAUGHT, BUT AT LEAST SHE'S NOT *BLAMING* HERSELF ANYMORE.

THE DOC SHOULDN'T. LIKE I SAID, THIS WAS ALL ME--*MY* DECISION.

I WANTED-- NAH, *NEEDED*-- TA DO IT.

BEN... *WHY*?

BELIEVE ME, I'M GRATEFUL--YOU SAVED LOWER MANHATTAN FROM DESTRUCTION-- BUT...YOU WERE *CURED*, FRIEND, WHY DID YOU DO IT?

... STRING-BEAN NEEDS HIS WING-MAN.

OH, BEN...

PLEASE DON'T SAY YOU DID THIS FOR ME.

... SINCE COLLEGE, I'VE *ALWAYS* WATCHED OUT FER YOU, REED, MAKING SURE YER EGGHEAD NEVER GOT *CRACK'D*...

HARD ENOUGH TA DO WHEN YA WEREN'T FIGHTING SUPER FISH CREEPS WHO C'N FLY...

THAT'S WHAT I *KNOW*, IT'S WHAT I *DO*...

NOW, IT'S THE SAME, JUST-- *BIGGER STAKES*. PLUS SUSIE AND JOHNNY ARE IN THE MIX...

"THERE'S A REASON THE FOUR OF US WENT INTA SPACE TOGETHER AND CAME BACK LIKE WE DID...

"A REASON *I* CAME BACK LIKE I DID...

"AND IT *WASN'T* SO I COULD LET MY PEEPS RISK THEIR LIVES WHILE I KICK BACK WITH A BREWSKIE AND THE GIANTS ON SUNDAY AFTERNOONS..."

I APPRECIATE WHAT YOU'RE SAYING, BEN, BUT WE COULD-- *WE CAN*--TRY TO MAKE YOU HUMAN AGAIN--

SURE WE C'N *TRY*, AND PROB'LY I'LL WANT YA TO, EVENTUALLY, BUT FOR RIGHT NOW, REED...

...THIS IS *BIGGER* THAN US. THIS IS HOW IT'S *SUPPOSED* TA BE.

The Beginning!

DNA-BASED PROCESSING. REDUNDANT INTELLIGENCE CENTERS. TRANSUNIVERSAL POINT-TO-POINT DATA STREAMING...

REALLY SOLID WORK, DR. WITTMAN.

OH! HERE'S THE REAL PROBLEM.

HUNTER-KILLER CLONES DESIGNED SPECIFICALLY TO TERMINATE US AND YOU'VE FOUND A *BIGGER PROBLEM*?

HE'S GOT A PLUTONIUM-POWERED BRAIN, SUE.

HE'S HIS OWN *FINAL SOLUTION.*

GREAT. ANY OTHER BAD NEWS?

BOMB'S ACTIVE.

I CAN TRACK THE FEED. UNFORTUNATELY I ONLY PACKED A SINGLE TRANSLOCATOR. DON'T WORRY, THIS SHOULDN'T TAKE LONG.

I'LL BE HOME FOR *DINNER.*

REED!

PLOOP!

HUH?

YES! POW! TAKE *THAT* BAD GUYS!

HA!

AND *THAT*... IS WHAT DADDY DID AT WORK TODAY.

TELL US ANOTHER STORY, DAD!

IT'S BEDTIME, FRANKLIN.

AND TONIGHT WAS AN EXCEPTION-- YOU KNOW THAT I DON'T LIKE STORY TIME TO BE ABOUT WHATEVER ADVENTURES YOUR MOTHER AND I GET INTO.

YOU HEAR ENOUGH ABOUT THAT FROM UNCLE JOHNNY AND BEN.

SO, TOMORROW NIGHT IT'S BACK TO READING FROM THE STRUCTURE OF SCIENTIFIC REVOLUTIONS. *EXCITING* STUFF.

AWWW, MAN.

GOOD NIGHT, VAL.

I HOPE THE PART ABOUT THE BOMBS DIDN'T SCARE YOU.

DAD, I KNOW THAT YOU REBUILT THE ENTIRE TOP OF THE BUILDING TO ACT AS AN INTERDIMENSIONAL PANIC ROOM.

I WASN'T AFRAID-- FRANKLIN AND I WERE FINE.

BESIDES, I'M THREE YEARS OLD-- IT'S IMPORTANT FOR ME NOT TO SPEND TIME THINKING ABOUT THINGS LIKE THAT.

'NIGHT!

HE TOOK THREE DAYS LONGER THAN NORMAL.

IT'S TO BE EXPECTED.

HE'S A TROUBLED AND CONFLICTED MAN.

HOW CAN WE HELP YOU, REED RICHARDS?

HOW DO I SOLVE EVERYTHING?

"CLASSIC"

"BYRNE"

"REAL WORLD"

COSTUME DESIGNS

REED RICHARDS

"FLIGHT SUIT"

NO BELT   "BELTED"

SUE STORM

James Dean/
Young Brad Pitt?

JOHNNY STORM

BENJAMIN GRIMM

"CLASSIC"   "BYRNE"   "REAL WORLD"

COSTUME DESIGNS

REED RICHARDS

"FLIGHT" SUIT

NO BELT   "BELTED"

SUE STORM

James Dean/
young Brad Pitt ?

JOHNNY STORM

BENJAMIN GRIMM